The
BACHELOR
TRIVIA
Game Book

*Note: This book contains questions about
"The Bachelor" franchise through the year 2021.*

What you need

- This book!
- 2-6 players
- A smartphone timer or stopwatch
- Scoring method (Pen and paper, or smartphone)

How to play

Choose a person to keep score.

General trivia questions are worth 1, 2 or 3 points based on difficulty. Although "The Bachelor" contestant last names are sometimes included in this book, players only need to provide the first name for a correct answer.

The youngest player reads the first question to the player directly to his or her right. If the player answers correctly, he or she earns the number of points for that question. (Correct answers can be found on the page that follows each question.) The youngest player passes the book to the person on his or her left, who then asks the next question to the youngest player. Continue moving the book around your group in this fashion.

If only two players, simply pass the book back and forth.

If a player lands on a bonus round page, that person will have an opportunity to earn up to 6 points. Some of these questions involve a time limit. Read all instructions aloud when landing on a bonus round page, and use a timer when necessary. The question reader should keep track of correct answers in a bonus round, and tally the points for the scorekeeper.

The player with the most points at the end wins. You may choose to play the entire book. For a shorter round, elect to end the game on page 50 or page 100, and pick up from there next time.

Question

Who was the very first
Bachelor on season 1?

Answer

Alex Michel

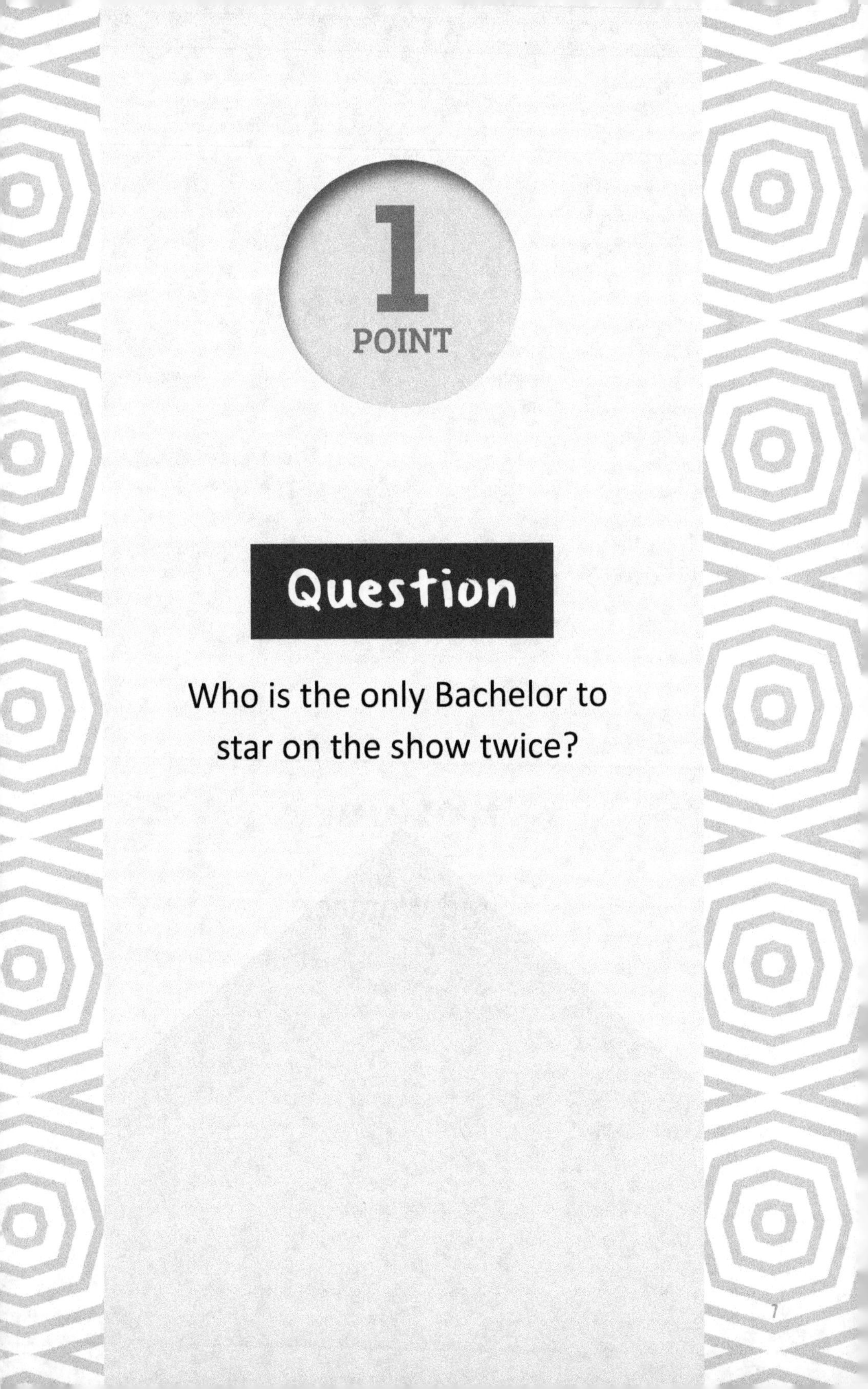

1
POINT

Question

Who is the only Bachelor to star on the show twice?

Answer

Brad Womack

Question

In what California city
is the Bachelor mansion?

Multiple choice:

1. Glendale
2. Los Angeles
3. Agoura Hills
4. San Diego

Answer

Agoura Hills

Question

In what season did Bachelor fans first hear "I'm not here to make friends"?

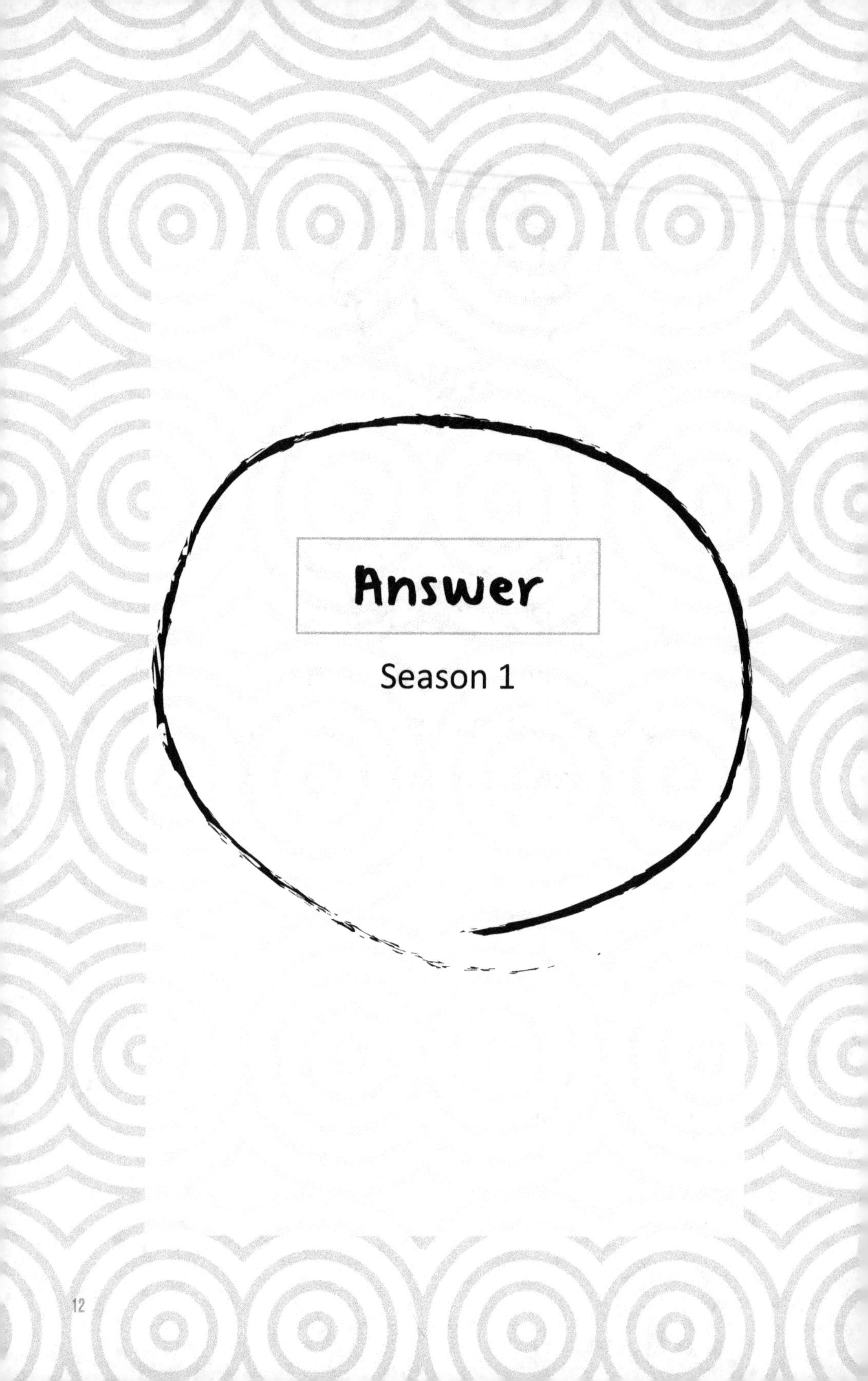
Answer
Season 1

BONUS
Round!

(No pressure or anything.)

BONUS Round!

You have 60 seconds to answer once the question is read aloud. Through 25 seasons, 4 people whose first names start with the letter J have starred as "The Bachelor." Name them. (One point for each name for a maximum of 4 points.)

Jesse Palmer
Jason Mesnick
Jake Pavelka
Juan Pablo Galavis

Question

Which Bachelor gave a woman a rose by accident because he couldn't remember her name?

Answer

Jesse Palmer

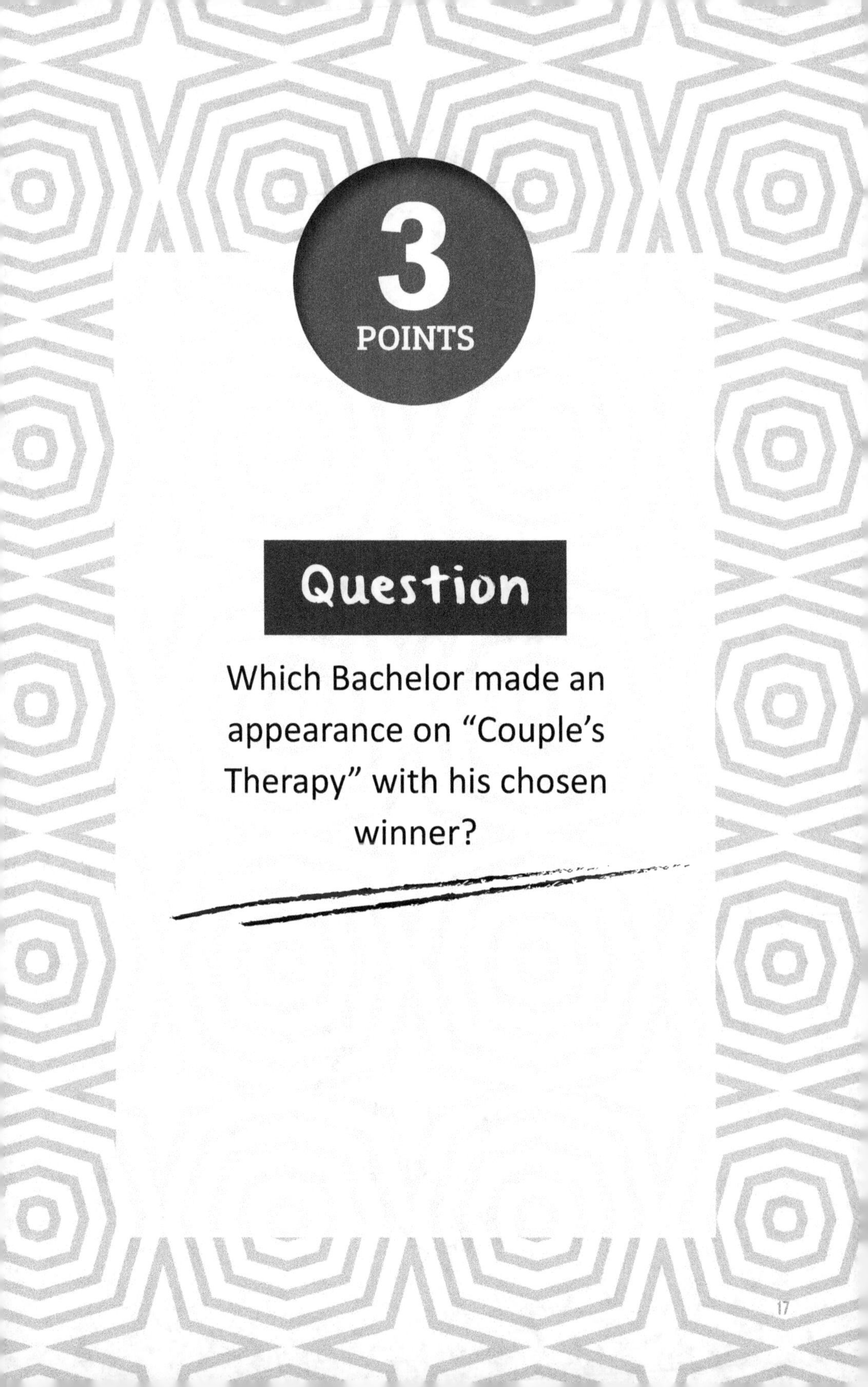

Question

Which Bachelor made an appearance on "Couple's Therapy" with his chosen winner?

Answer

Juan Pablo Galavis

Question

Victoria Larson called herself a "queen" and wore a tiara when she competed on whose season of "The Bachelor"?

Answer
Matt James

Question

What were the twins'
names on Ben Higgins'
season?

Answer

Emily and Haley

In whose country music video did Trista Sutter make an appearance in 2003?

Answer

Brad Paisley

2
POINTS

Question

Who got engaged on the
first season of "Bachelor In
Paradise"?

25

Answer

Marcus Grodd
and Lacy Faddoul

Question

What town in Iowa
is Bachelor Chris Soules
from?

Answer

Arlington

Question

Which of Chris Soules'
contestants kept talking
about aliens?

Answer

Ashley Salter

BONUS
Round!

(Big chance to prove your "Bachelor" love.)

BONUS Round!

The question reader will read six statements aloud concerning the arrival of former contestants to the Bachelor Mansion on night one. The guesser will decide if each statement is true or false.
(1 point for each correct answer for a maximum of 6 points.)

Statement 1: A contestant arrived in a sloth costume.
TRUE! Alex Dillon (Season: Colton Underwood)

Statement 2: A contestant arrived wearing a unicorn head.
TRUE! Jojo Fletcher (Season: Ben Higgins)

Statement 3: A contestant arrived dressed as Donald Trump.
FALSE! Nobody tried to Make the Bachelor Great Again.

Statement 4: A contestant rode in on a camel.
TRUE! Lacey Mark (Season: Nick Viall)

Statement 5: A contestant arrived riding a zebra.
FALSE! No zebras. Yet.

Statement 6: A contestant arrived as a giant paper airplane.
TRUE! Madison Prewett (Season: Peter Weber)

Question

What is Emily Maynard's oldest child's name?

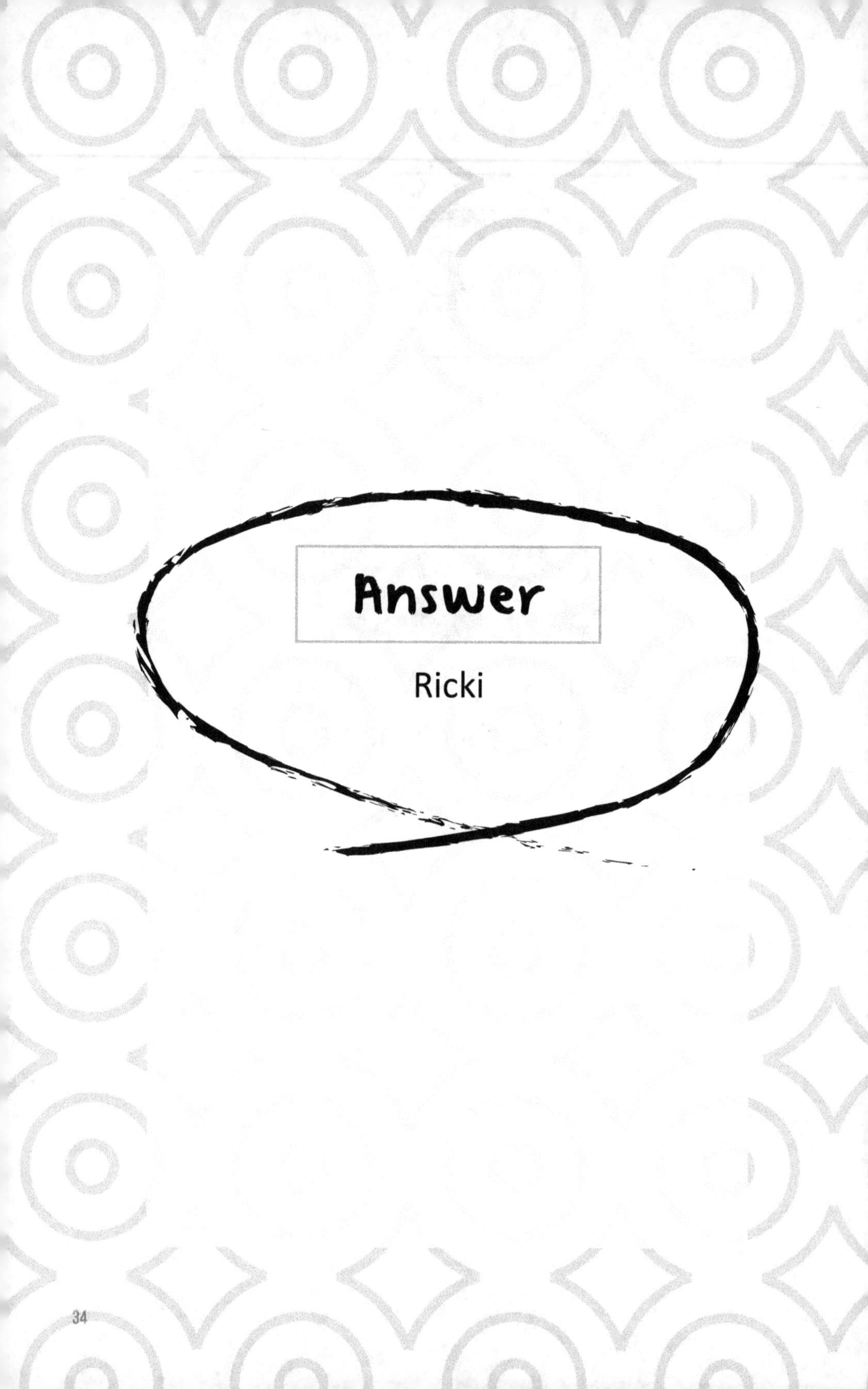

Answer
Ricki

Question

What is the title of contestant Courtney Robertson's book?

Answer

"I Didn't Come Here to Make Friends"

Question

What Bachelorette star famously said, "I'm not here to fix anybody. This isn't build-a-man workshop"?

Answer

Charity Lawson

Finish the "Bachelor In Paradise" theme song lyric: "Almost paradise..."

Answer

Either answer is acceptable:

"...we're knocking
on Heaven's door."

– or –

"How could we ask for more?"

Question

Two contestants were chosen from Matt James's season to star as the Bachelorette. Name one.

Answer

Katie Thurston and
Michelle Young

Question

What is the name of the
original bartender on
"Bachelor In Paradise?"

Answer

Jorge

Question

What male contestant from "The Bachelorette" was known for his stylish and bold earrings?

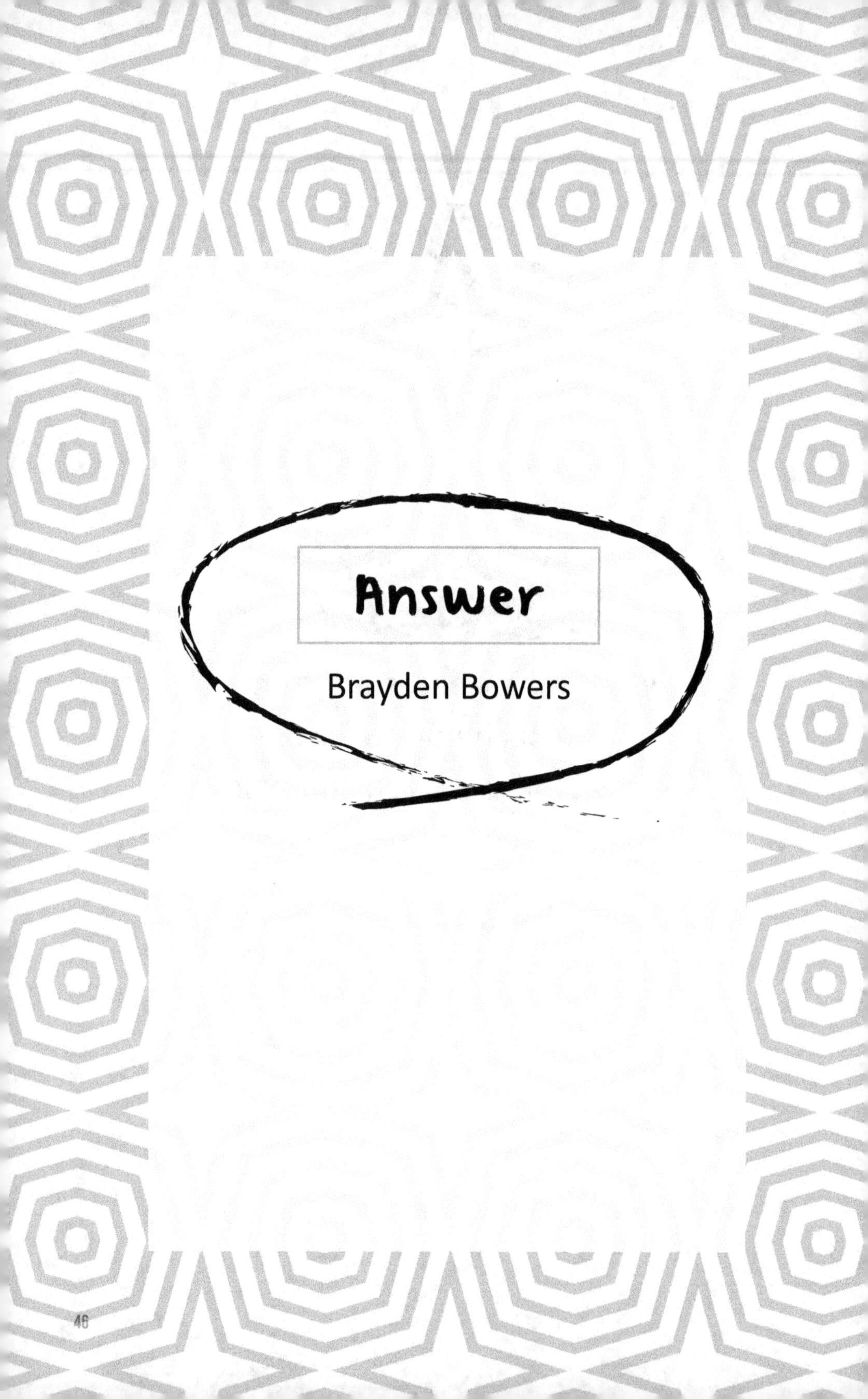

Answer
Brayden Bowers

Question

Which Bachelor contestant
talked about her nanny
making her cheesy pasta?

Answer

Corinne Olympios

Question

Who was the first ever
African-American to star as
Bachelor or Bachelorette?

Answer

Rachel Lindsey

What was the name of Ben Higgins and Lauren Bushnell's reality show?

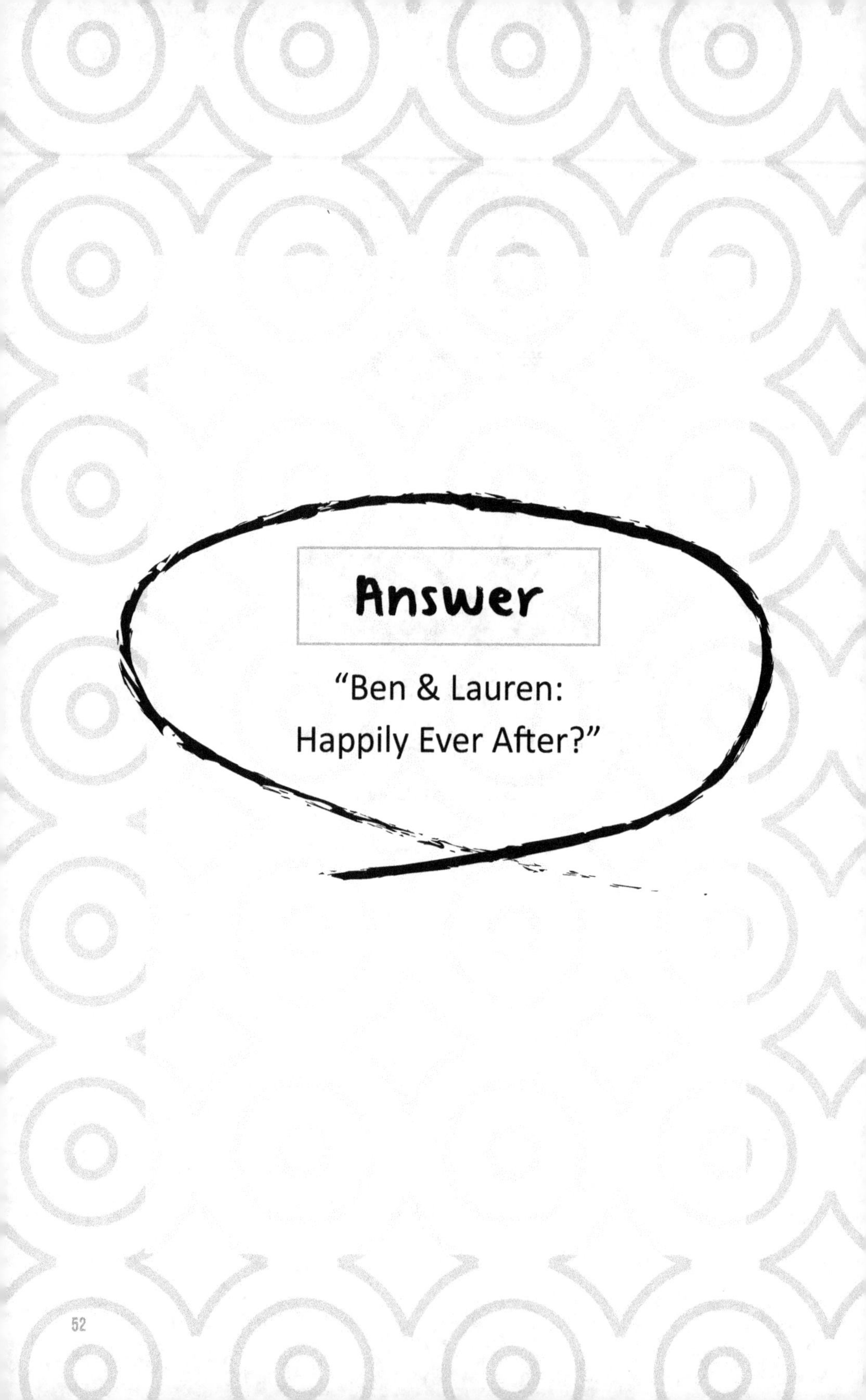
Answer

"Ben & Lauren:
Happily Ever After?"

BONUS Round!

(Take a moment, say your answer.)

BONUS Round!

The question reader will read the names of the
first five men to star as "The Bachelor." The guesser
will try to name the woman who finished as the
runner-up in each season. As always, only a first name
is needed for a correct answer. One guess per season.
(1 point for each name for a maximum of 5 points.)

Season 1: Alex Michel   **Runner-up:** Trista Rehn
Season 2: Aaron Buerge   **Runner-up:** Brooke Smith
Season 3: Andrew Firestone   **Runner-up:** Kirsten Buschbacher
Season 4: Bob Guiney   **Runner-up:** Kelly Jo Kuarski
Season 5: Jesse Palmer   **Runner-up:** Tara Huckeby

Question

Who is the series creator and producer behind "The Bachelor" franchise?

Answer

Mike Fleiss

Question

Which show contestant
has been runner-up in the
Final Two twice?

Answer

Nick Viall

Question

Who did Kaitlyn Bristowe
compete with to star on
"The Bachelorette"?

Answer

Britt Nilsson

Question

Who was the runner-up
on Zach Shallcross's season?

Answer

Gabi Elnicki

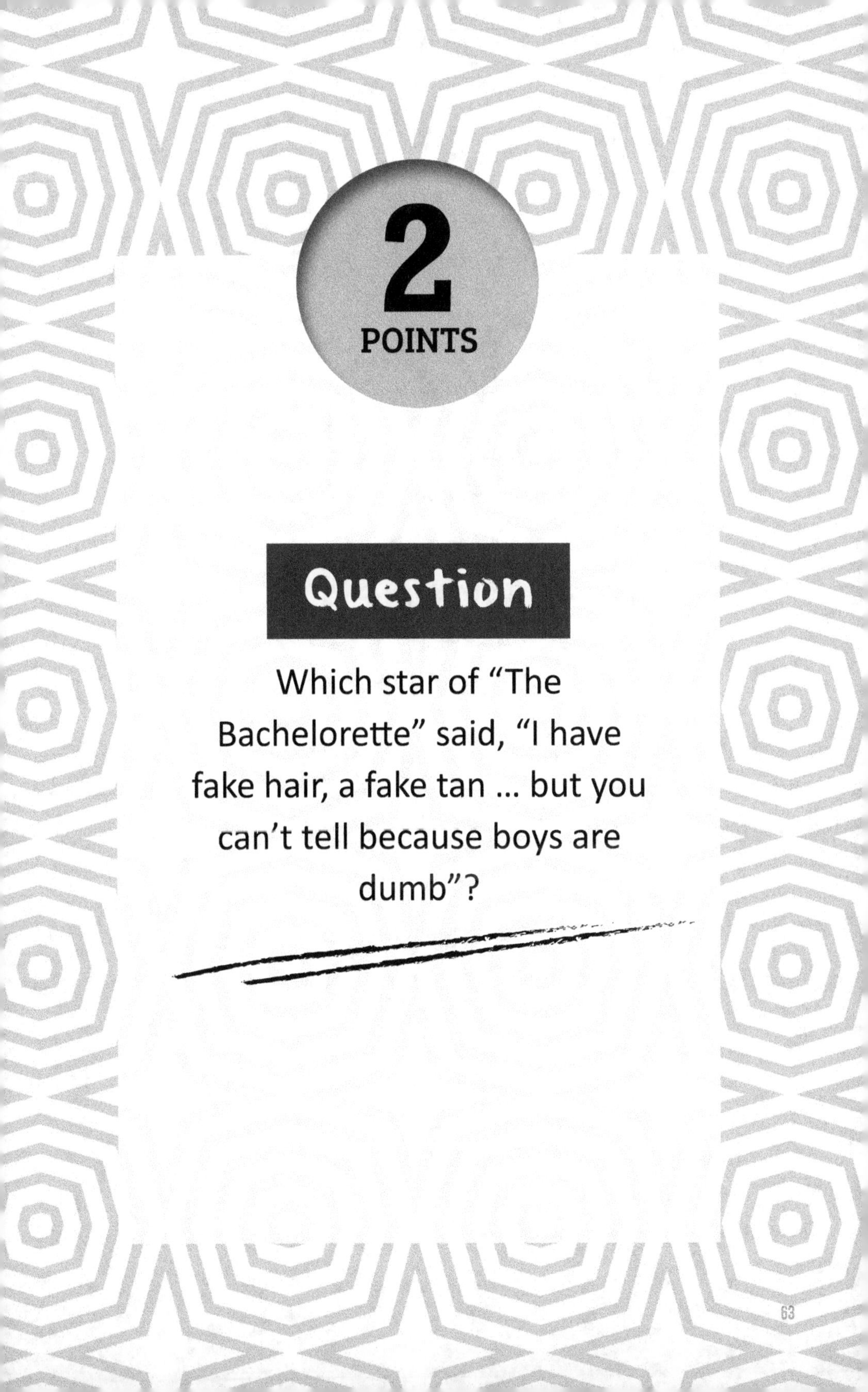

2
POINTS

Question

Which star of "The Bachelorette" said, "I have fake hair, a fake tan ... but you can't tell because boys are dumb"?

Answer

Gabby Windey

Question

What's the name of
Andi Dorfman's book?

Answer
"It's Not Okay"

BONUS
Round!

(Don't play to make friends.)

BONUS Round!

Who am I?

The three statements below apply to one specific contestant on "The Bachelor." You may take one guess after each statement is read.

Correct guess after one statement: 5 points
Correct guess after two statements: 4 points
Correct guess after three statements: 3 points

Statement 1: She refused to attend the second half of a group date after she felt the Bachelor broke a promise.
Statement 2: She was accused of talking with a fake baby voice.
Statement 3: She later won season 5 of "Bachelor in Paradise" and got engaged on the show finale.

ANSWER: Krystal Nielsen

Who did Jason Mesnick dump
in order to get back together
with his runner-up?

Answer

Melissa Rycroft

Question

Which contestant was accused of "engaging in an inappropriate relationship" with one of the producers on Jake Pavelka's season?

Answer

Rozlyn Papa

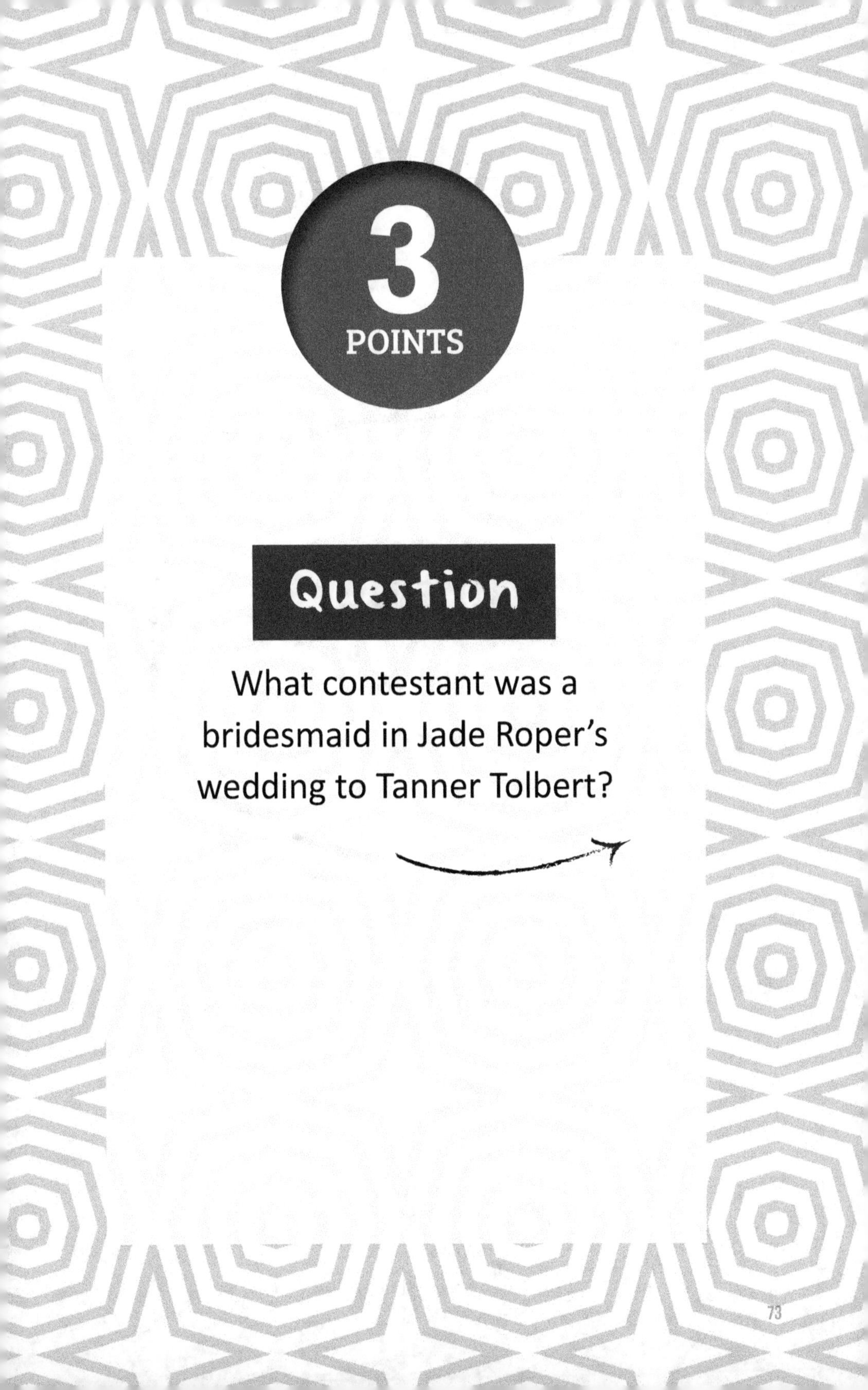

Question

What contestant was a bridesmaid in Jade Roper's wedding to Tanner Tolbert?

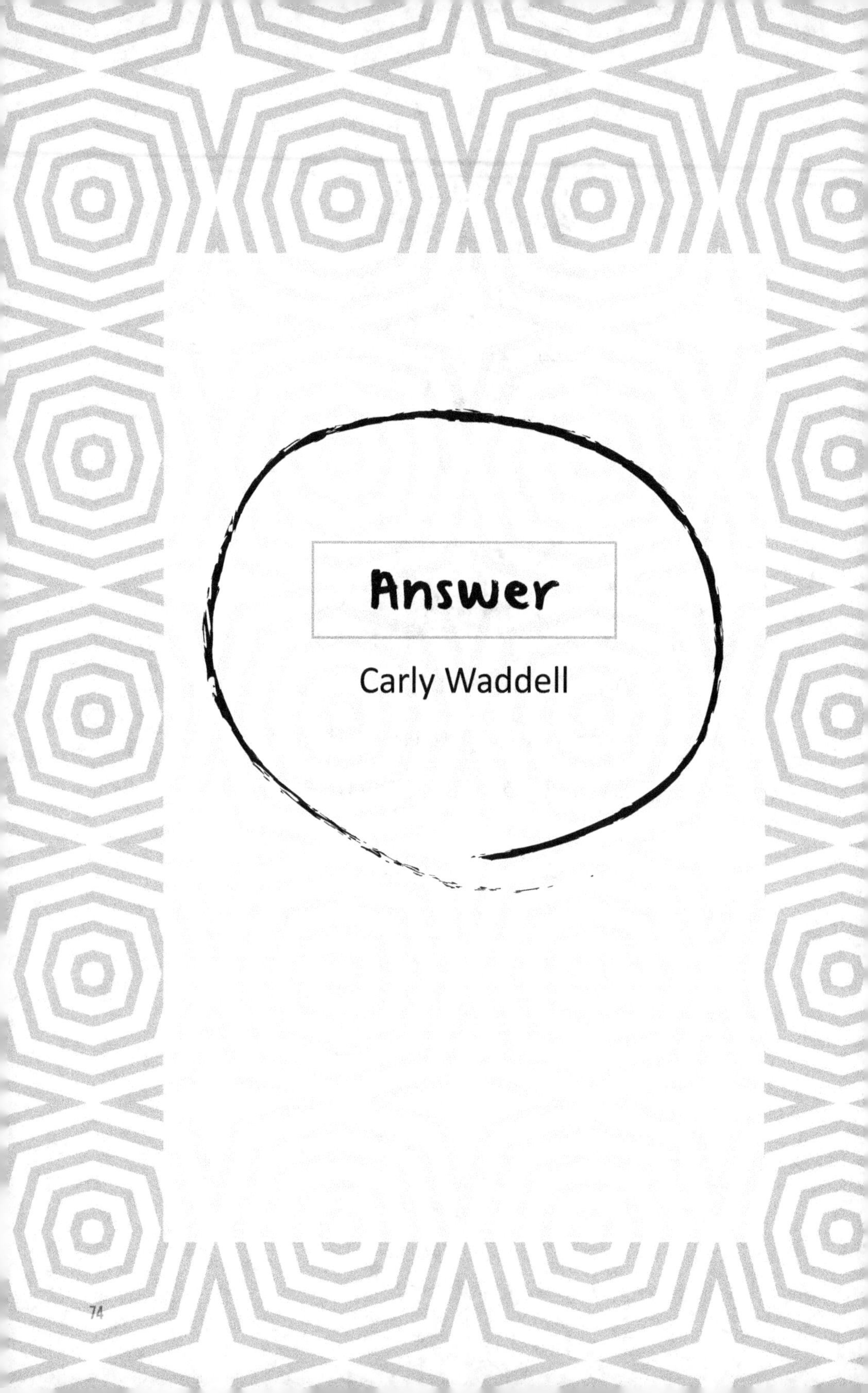

Answer
Carly Waddell

Question

Who was the oldest person
to star on "The Bachelor"?

Answer

Byron Velvick
(Age: 40)

Who said he was the first guy
on "The Bachelorette"
to "make it to the top four
with a girlfriend?"

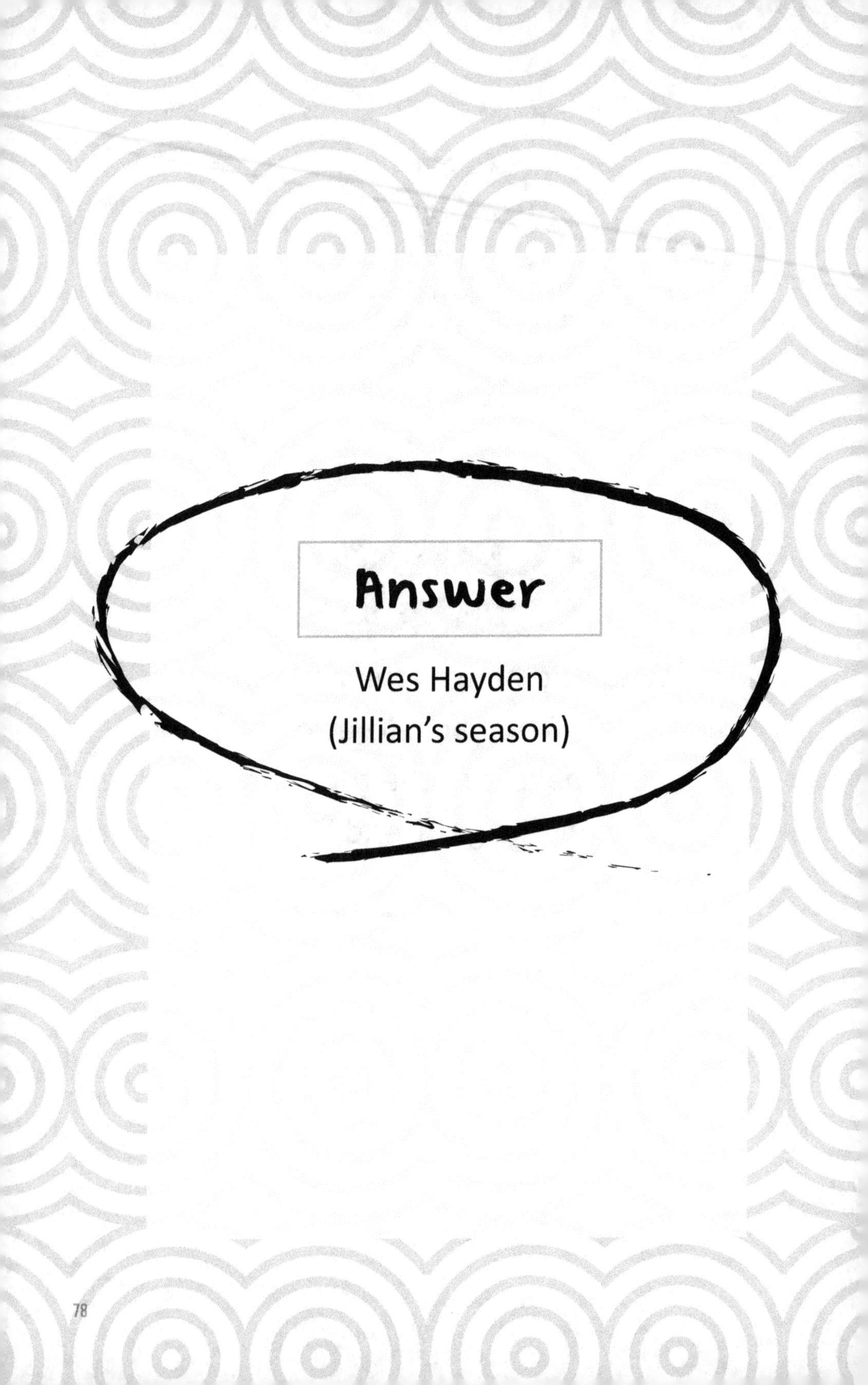

Answer

Wes Hayden
(Jillian's season)

Question

Who quit Jake Pavelka's
season so she wouldn't lose
her job and later starred as
Bachelorette?

Answer

Ali Fedotowsky

Question

Which couple who got
engaged on "The Bachelor"
later had their own
break-up special?

Answer

Jake Pavelka and
Vienna Giardi

Question

Which two contestants
famously went skinny dipping
in Puerto Rico?

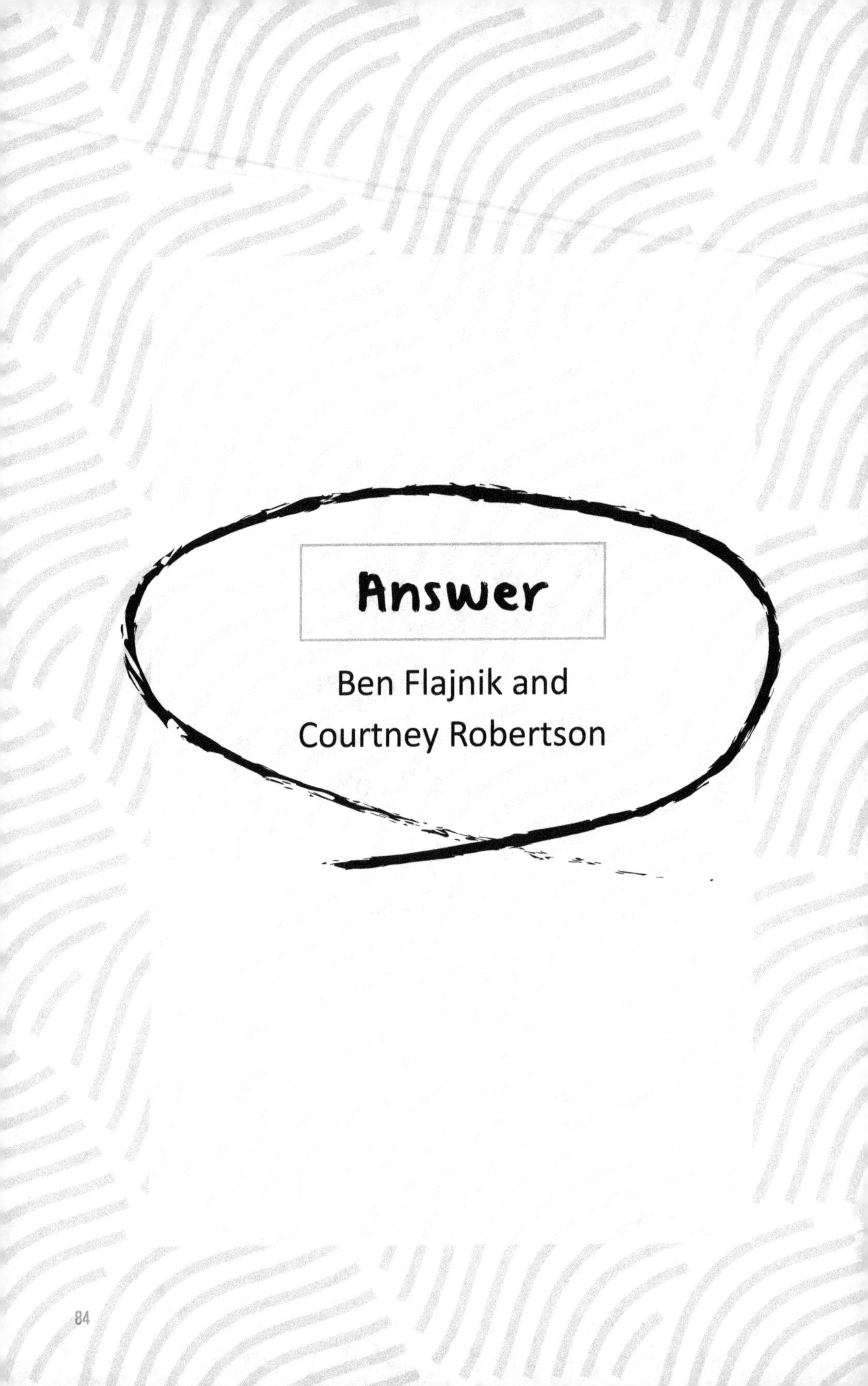

Answer

Ben Flajnik and
Courtney Robertson

BONUS
Round!

(This is all part of your journey.)

BONUS Round!

Two stars from "The Bachelor" and two stars
from "The Bachelorette" had their weddings broadcast
as a television special. Name them.
(1 point for each correct name for a maximum of 4 points.)

Trista Rehn
Jason Mesnick
Ashley Hebert
Sean Lowe

Question

What runner-up from Sean Lowe's season took off her heels as she walked away after being rejected by him in the finale?

Answer

Lindsay Yenter

Question

Which contestant on "The Bachelorette" was known not only for a temper and aggressive behavior, but biting a raw sweet potato?

Answer

Chad Johnson

1
POINT

Question

What star of "The Bachelor"
later came out as gay?

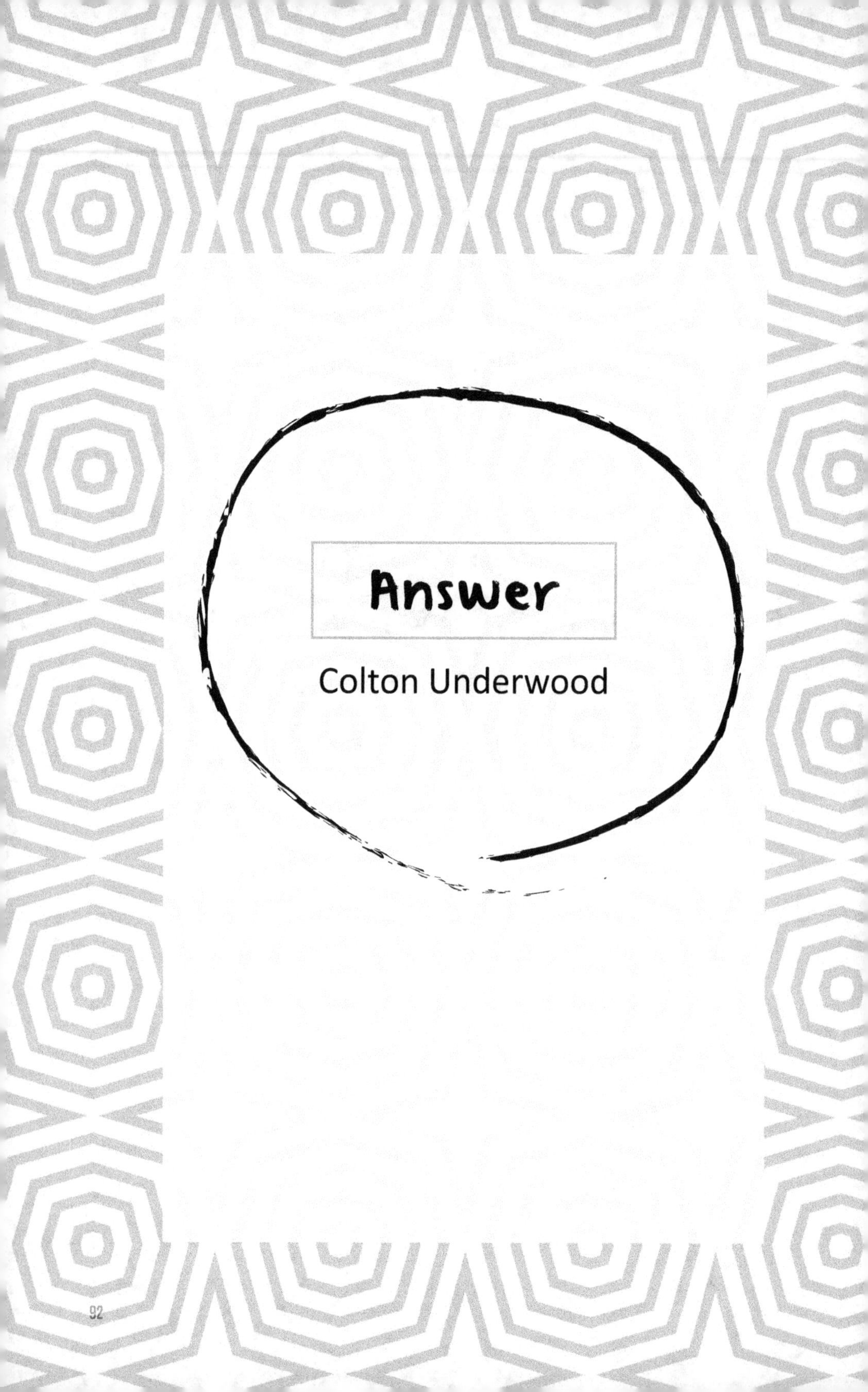

Answer
Colton Underwood

Who slapped the star of "The Bachelor" across the face when she first met him after coming out of the limo?

Answer

Chantal O'Brien
(She slapped Brad Womack for
not picking either woman in
his first Bachelor run)

BONUS
Round!

(It's harder than a group date.)

BONUS Round!

The question reader will read five statements aloud about "The Bachelor." The guesser will decide if each statement is true or false.
(1 point for each correct answer for a maximum of 5 points.)

Statement 1: Jimmy Kimmel created a parody of the show called "The Little Bachelor."
FALSE! It was called "The Baby Bachelor" and starred his three-year-old nephew.

Statement 2: "The Bachelor Summer Games" premiered in 2020.
FALSE! It was scheduled, but cancelled due to COVID-19.

Statement 3: In season 6, the women decided who would be "The Bachelor" after meeting two men.
TRUE! Byron Velvick was selected over Jay Overbye.

Statement 4: Producers make contestants use the word "journey."
TRUE! Scenes have been rerecorded to include the magic word.

Statement 5: Each female gets a $500 stipend for clothes.
FALSE! Women must buy their own clothes for the show.

Question

Kalon McMahon arrived to Emily Maynard's season of "The Bachelorette" using what type of transportation?

Answer

Helicopter

2
POINTS

Question

Who was the first woman
from Canada to star on
"The Bachelorette"?

Answer

Jillian Harris

Question

What famous Bachelor virgin later appeared on "Bachelor in Paradise" and eventually married Jared Haibon after meeting him there?

Answer

Ashley Ioncentti

Question

What tennis instructor was named as "The Bachelor" in 2023 after failing to win Charity Lawson's heart?

<table><tr><td>

Answer

</td></tr></table>

Joey Graziadei

BONUS
Round!

(Your odds are better here than on a 2-on-1 date.)

BONUS Round!

Who am I?

The three statements below apply to one specific contestant on "The Bachelor." You may take one guess after each statement is read.

Correct guess after one statement: 5 points
Correct guess after two statements: 4 points
Correct guess after three statements: 3 points

Statement 1: She was part of a Final Two in which neither woman was selected.
Statement 2: She later dated contestant John Paul Jones.
Statement 3: She eventually stepped in as "The Bachelorette" when the original choice ended her season early.

ANSWER: Tayshia Adams

Question

What state is Gerry Turner from, the first "Golden Bachelor"?

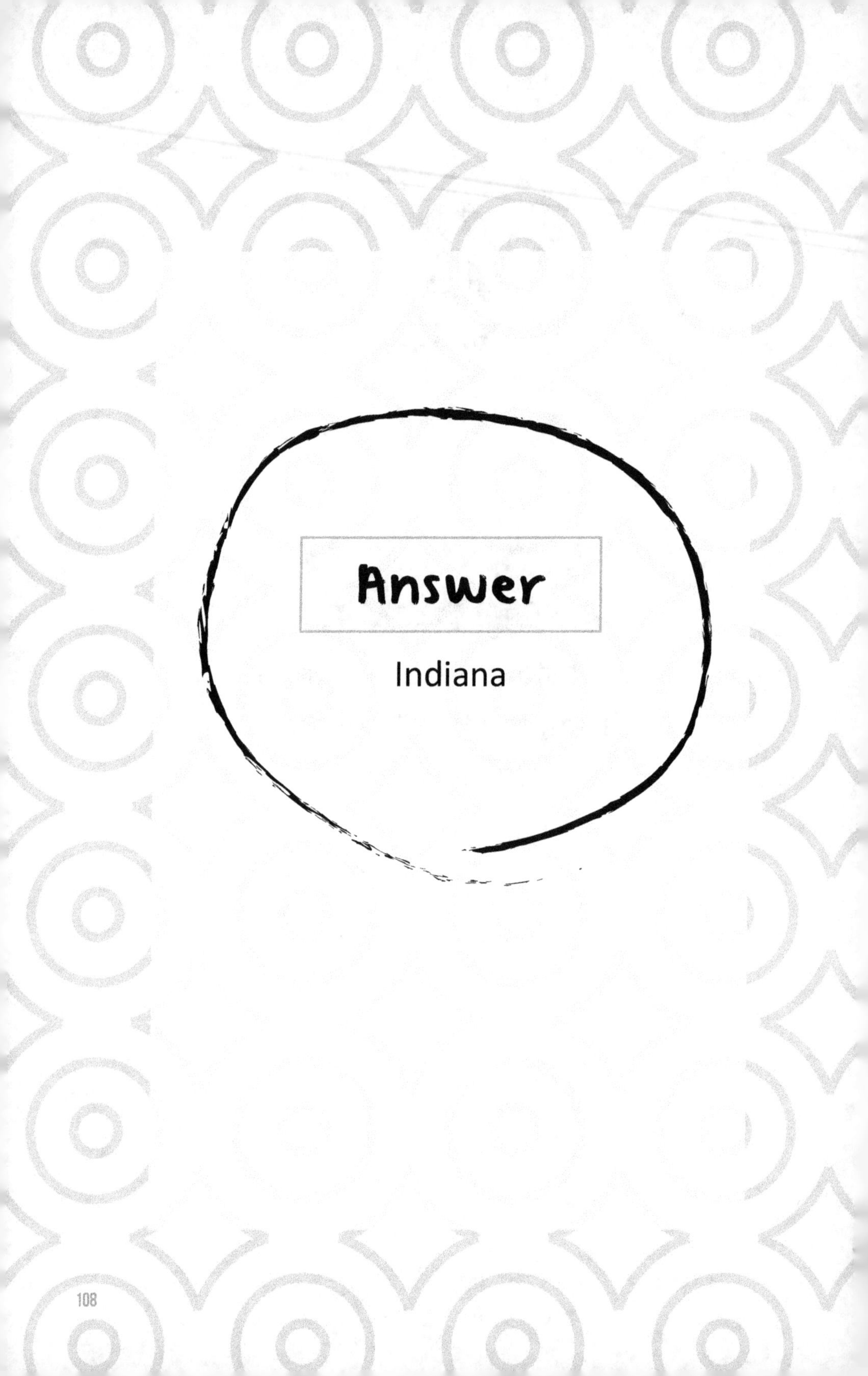
Answer
Indiana

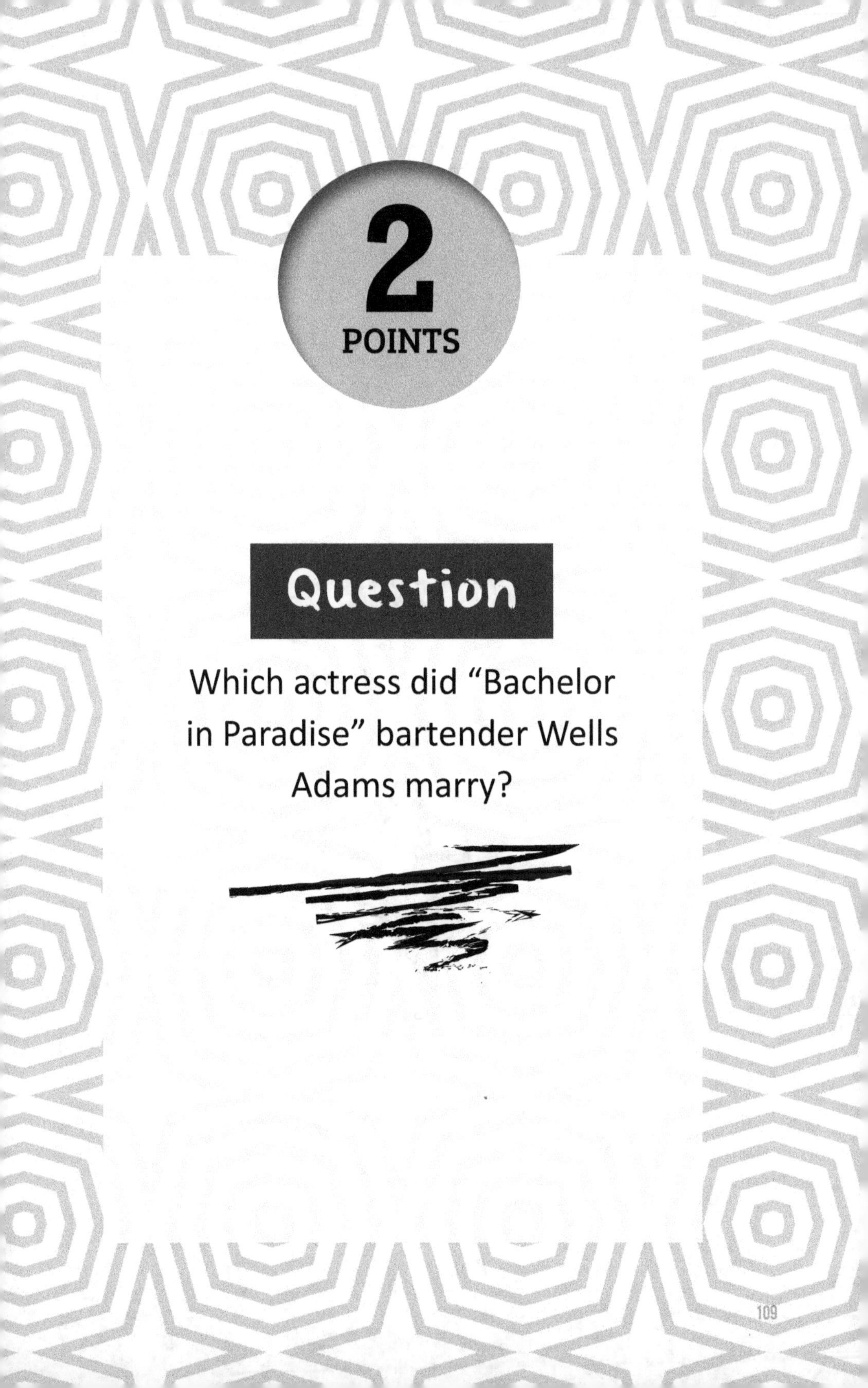

2 POINTS

Question

Which actress did "Bachelor in Paradise" bartender Wells Adams marry?

Answer

Sarah Hyland

Question

Johnny DePhillipo was briefly engaged to whom after season 8 of "Bachelor in Paradise"?

Answer

Victoria Fuller

Question

Which star of "The Bachelor" married a soap opera star after his romance from the show fizzled?

Answer

Bob Guiney

BONUS
Round!

(Play for the right reasons.)

BONUS Round!

Through 16 seasons of "The Bachelorette," six stars have given their First Impression Roses to the man they eventually chose in the Final Rose Ceremony. Name the bachelorettes.
Note: You get only six guesses.
(1 point for each name for a maximum of 6 points.)

DeAnna Pappas   (Jesse Csincsak)
Ali Fedotowsky   (Roberto Martinez)
Kaitlyn Bristowe   (Shawn Booth)
JoJo Fletcher   (Jordan Rodgers)
Rachel Lindsay   (Bryan Abasolo)
Becca Kufrin   (Garrett Yrigoyen)

Question

Bachelor Arie Luyendyk Jr. later competed on what Peacock reality show?

Answer

"The Traitors"

Question

In what year did "The Bachelor" first premiere in the United States?

Answer

2002

Question

In what year did "Bachelor in Paradise" premiere?

Answer
2014

Question

True or false: Through the first
22 seasons of "The Bachelor,"
exactly half of them ended
with an official proposal.

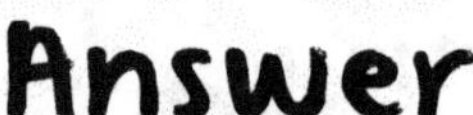

Answer

False
(14 of the first 22 seasons
ended with a proposal)

POINTS

Who had the first televised
wedding from the franchise?

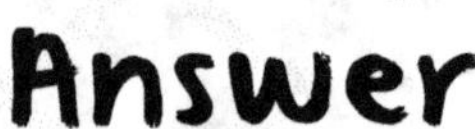

Answer

Trista Rehn and Ryan Sutter

Question

What actor produced a
spin-off spoof of
"The Bachelor" called
"Burning Love"?

Answer

Ben Stiller

BONUS
Round!

(You know you want this rose.)

BONUS Round!

Read each question about the most horrible hometown dates in the history of "The Bachelor" and "The Bachelorette"! The guesser may give one answer per question.
(1 point for each correct answer for a maximum of 4 points.)

Who was asked to bury a dead bird after a contestant's mother said she had hit a bird with her car and stored it in her freezer?

Answer: Jason Mesnick

Who had to awkwardly watch as a hometown date performed a solo lyrical dance?

Answer: Jake Pavelka

Who's ex showed up to say that one of the hometown dates was responsible for breaking up other marriages?

Answer: Peter Weber

Who had to view a taxidermy collection belonging to a contestant's father?

Answer: Ali Fedotowsky

Question

True or false: Versions of "The Bachelor" have aired in more than 30 countries.

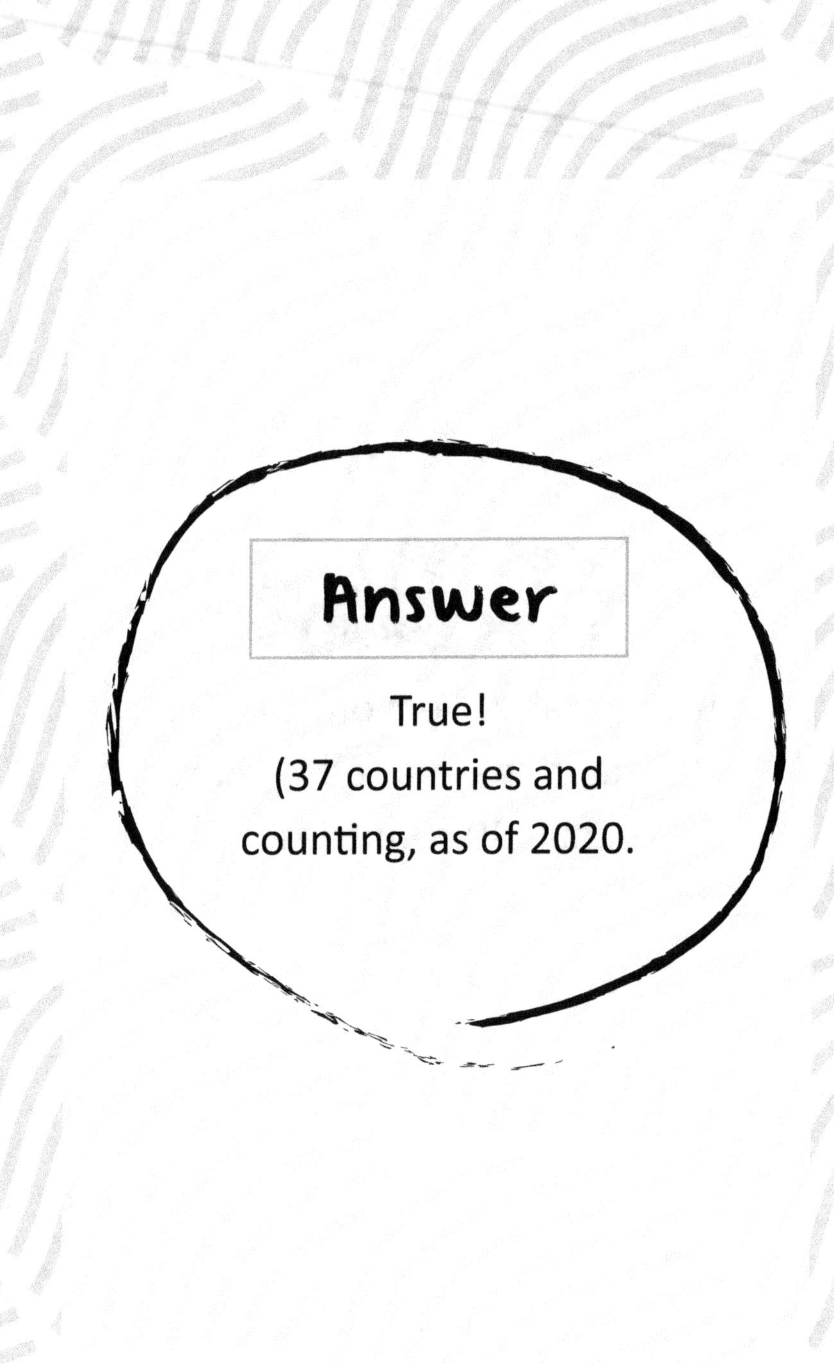

Answer
True!
(37 countries and
counting, as of 2020.

Question

Trista Rehn was the first star
of "The Bachelorette"
to officially marry her final
choice. Who was the second?

Answer

Ashley Herbert
(She married
J.P. Rosenbaum, although
they later separated.)

Question

Which controversial Bachelor contestant was left alone on a beach in Ben Higgins' season after getting eliminated on a two-on-one date?

Answer

Olivia Caridi

3
POINTS

Question

Bachelor Chris Soules took frequent crier Ashley I. and villain Kesley on a two-on-date in the desert. Who went home?

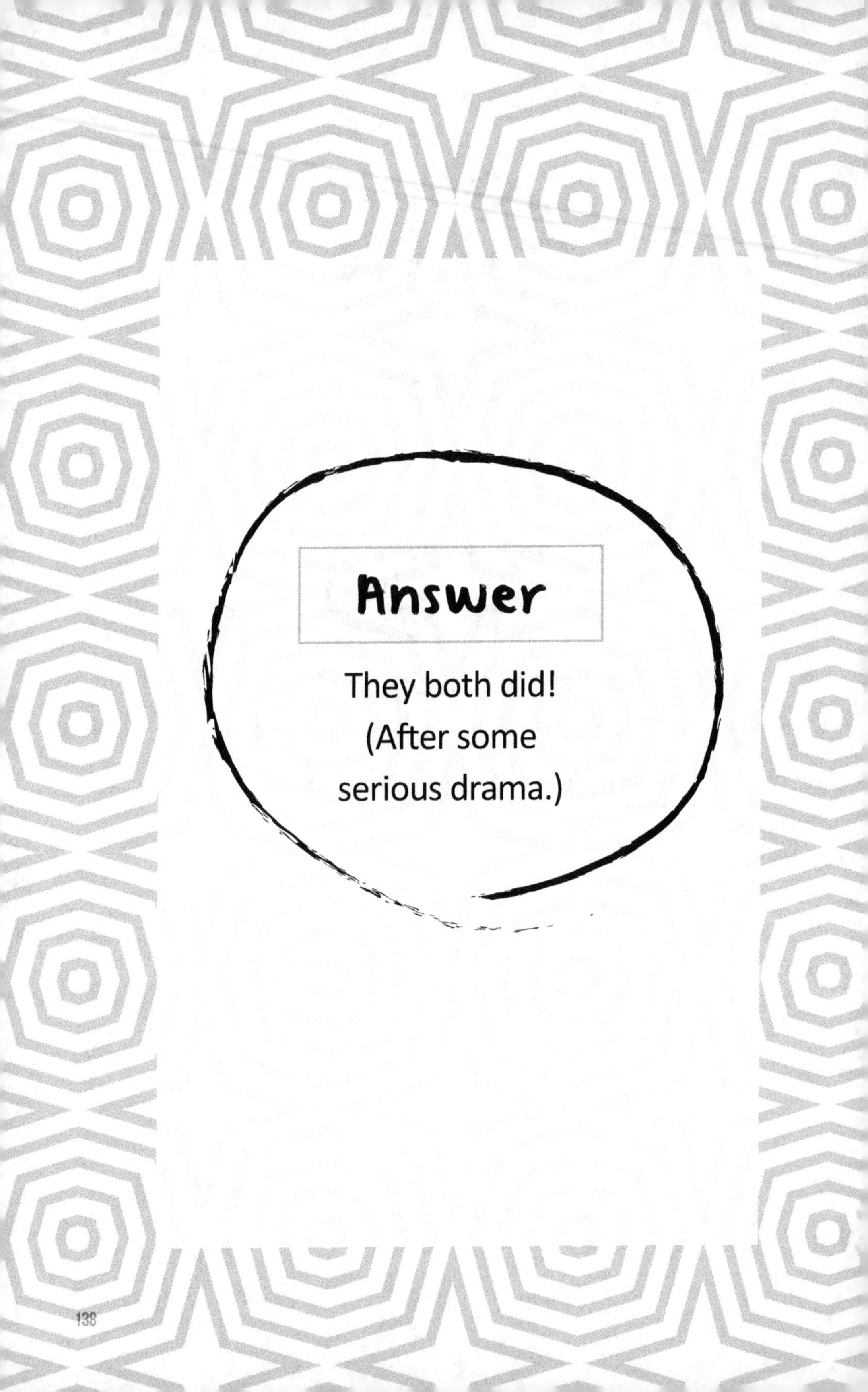

Answer

They both did!
(After some
serious drama.)

Question

Which female contestant
dated a woman on
"Bachelor in Paradise"?

Answer

Demi Burnett

After hosting "The Bachelor,"
Chris Harrison went on to host
a podcast with what name?

Answer

The Most Dramatic
Podcast Ever

Question

What male model contestant
wore gold hot pants on
Becca's season of
"The Bachelorette"?

Answer

Jordan Kimball

Question

Which contestant on
Bachelor Sean's season
referred to herself as having
"sparkle"?

Answer

Tierra LaCausi

Question

What country star appeared on Peter Weber's season and ended up performing for a woman he used to date?

Answer

Chase Rice

Question

What comedienne appeared
on Kaitlyn's Bachelorette
season to help the men write
their own comedy routines?

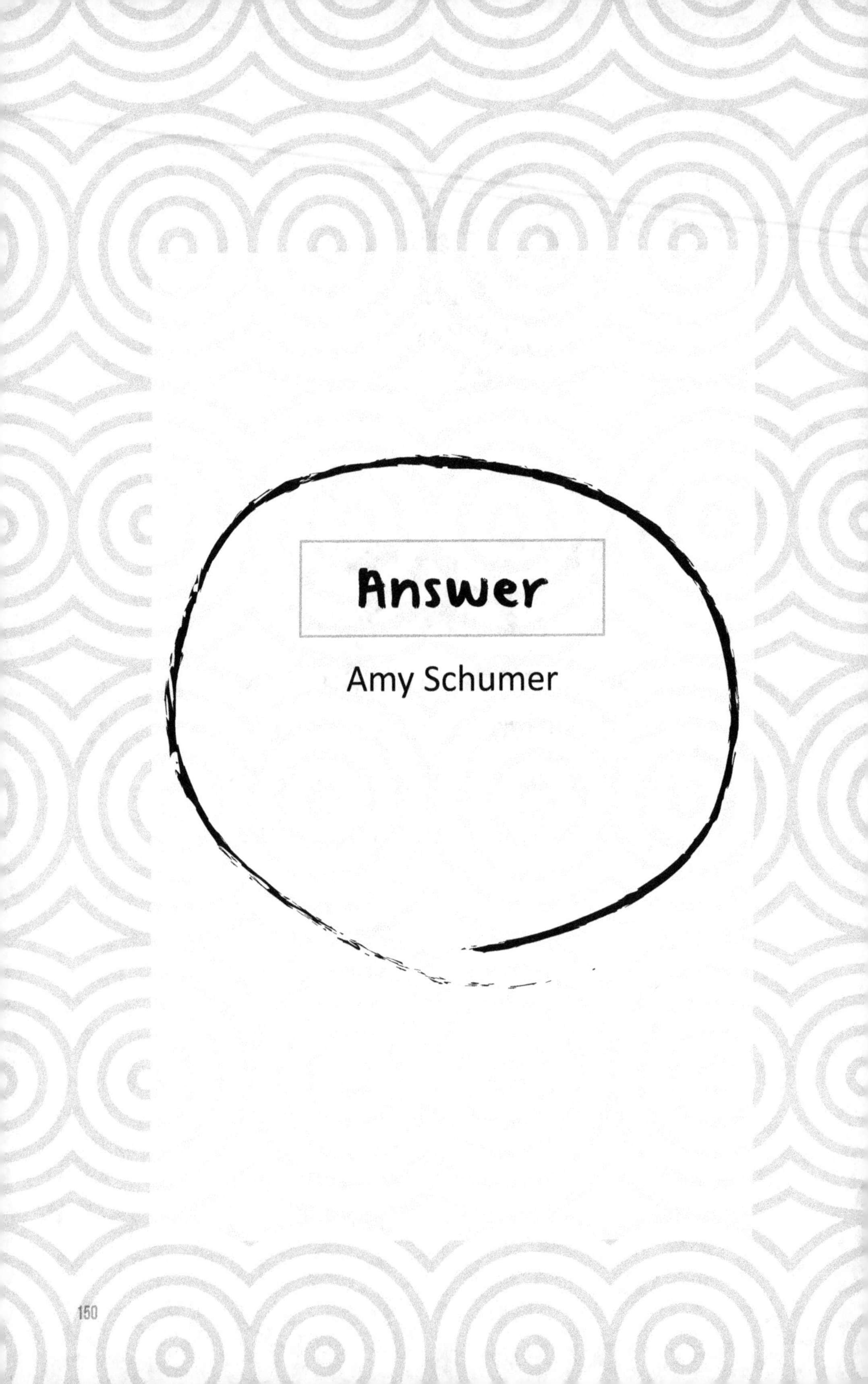
Answer
Amy Schumer

BONUS
Round!

(This is the Final. Round. Tonight.
Just kidding, there's more.)

BONUS Round!

Who am I?

The three statements below apply to one specific contestant on "The Bachelor." You may take one guess after each statement is read.

Correct guess after one statement: 5 points
Correct guess after two statements: 4 points
Correct guess after three statements: 3 points

Statement 1: She was a fan favorite on Sean Lowe's season.
Statement 2: She was paired with Robert Graham on "Bachelor in Paradise," but the relationship ended when he didn't want to get physical with her.
Statement 3: She was born with only one arm, and now helps other women feel confident through her non-profit SheLift.

ANSWER: Sarah Herron

Question

What contestant worked at a men's clinic helping patients with erectile dysfunction?

Answer

Evan Bass

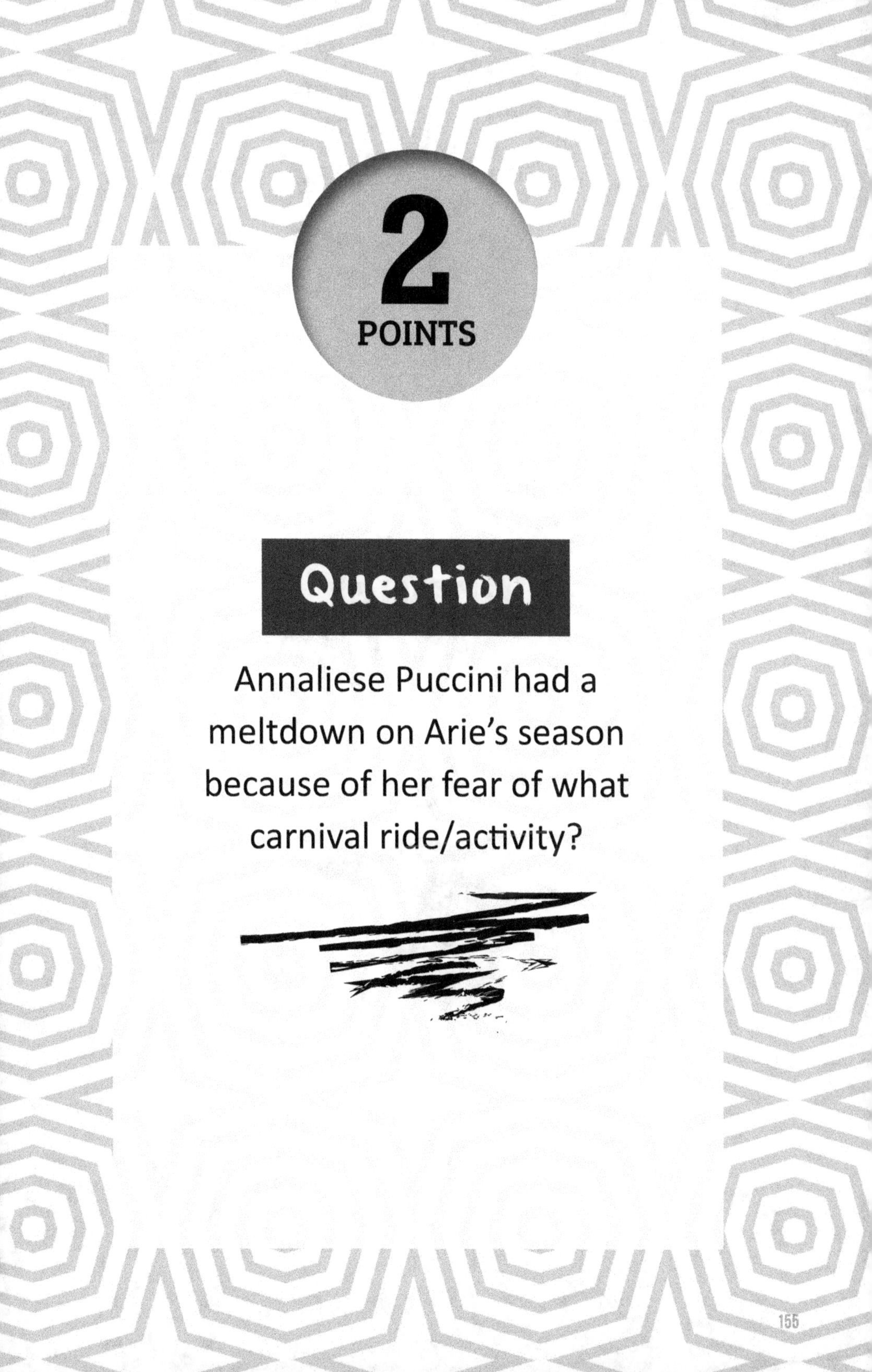

Question

Annaliese Puccini had a meltdown on Arie's season because of her fear of what carnival ride/activity?

Answer

Bumper cars

Question

What comedian appeared on Colton Underwood's season for a group date involving camp-themed games?

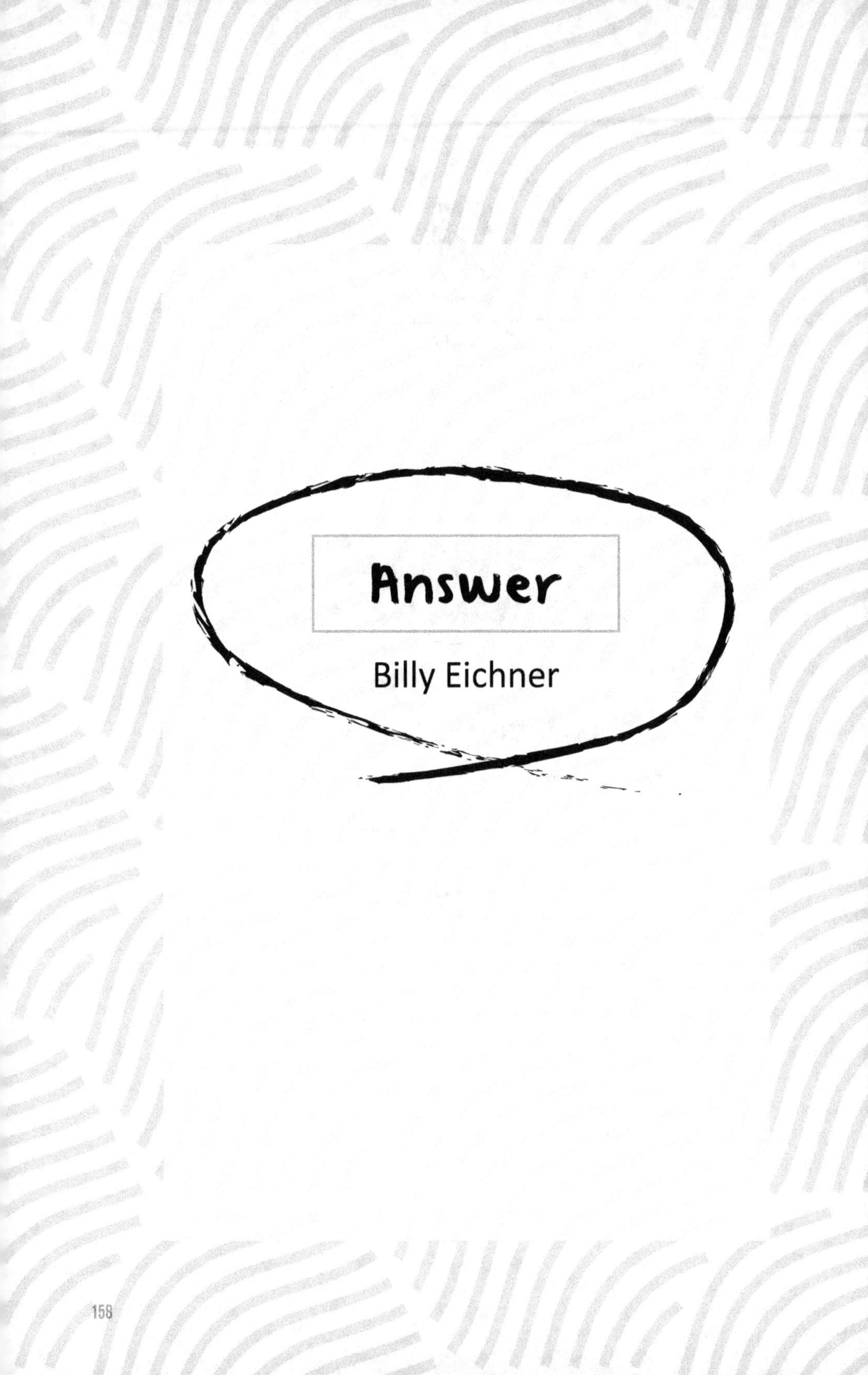

Answer

Billy Eichner

Question

Who vomited on a date with Nick Viall after they took a flight aboard a plane designed to simulate the feeling of weightlessness you get in space?

Answer

Vanessa Grimaldi

Question

Who arrived on night one of Juan Pablo's season wearing a pretend baby bump under her dress?

Answer

Clare Crawley

Question

What celebrity couple who starred on "That 70s Show" hosted an obstacle course on Rachel Lindsay's season?

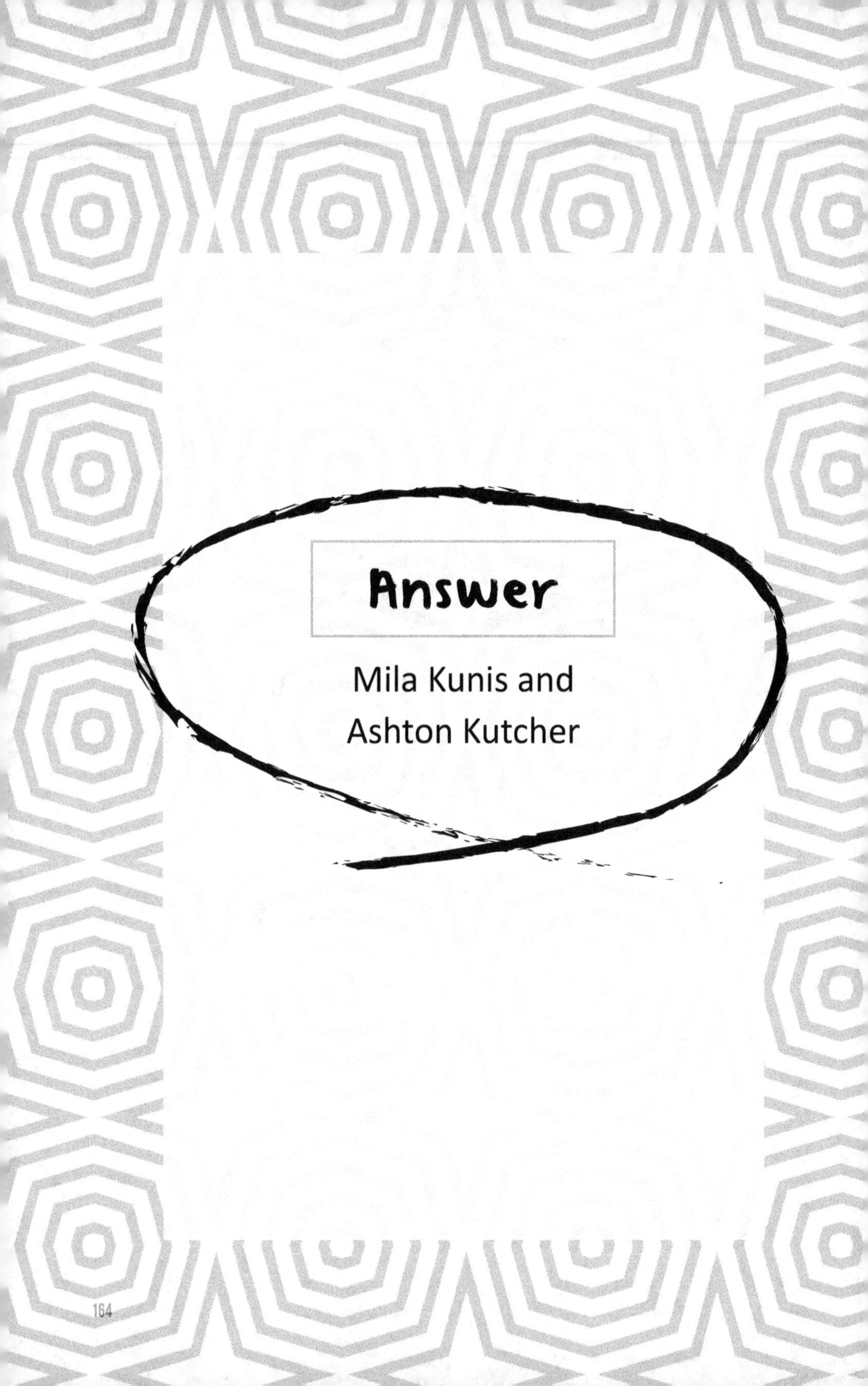

Answer

Mila Kunis and
Ashton Kutcher

Question

What contestant on Peter Weber's season accidentally sprayed herself in the face with champagne?

Answer

Kelsey Weier

What contestant wore a shark costume on night one to meet Bachelor Nick Viall? (She thought it was a dolphin costume!)

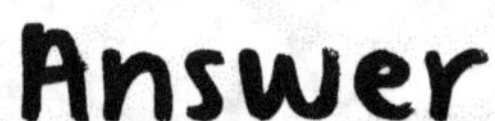

Answer

Alexis Waters

BONUS
Round!

(Hotter than a Fantasy Suite date.)

BONUS Round!

The question reader will read the names of five women who starred as "The Bachelorette." The guesser will try to name the man who finished as the runner-up in each season. As always, only a first name is needed for a correct answer. One guess per season.
(1 point for each name for a maximum of 5 points.)

Season 10: Andi Dorfman   **Runner-up:** Nick Viall
Season 11: Kaitlyn Bristowe   **Runner-up:** Nick Viall
Season 12: JoJo Fletcher   **Runner-up:** Robby Hayes
Season 13: Rachel Lindsay   **Runner-up:** Peter Kraus
Season 14: Becca Kufrin   **Runner-up:** Blake Hortsman

Question

Two pilots have starred on "The Bachelor." Name one.

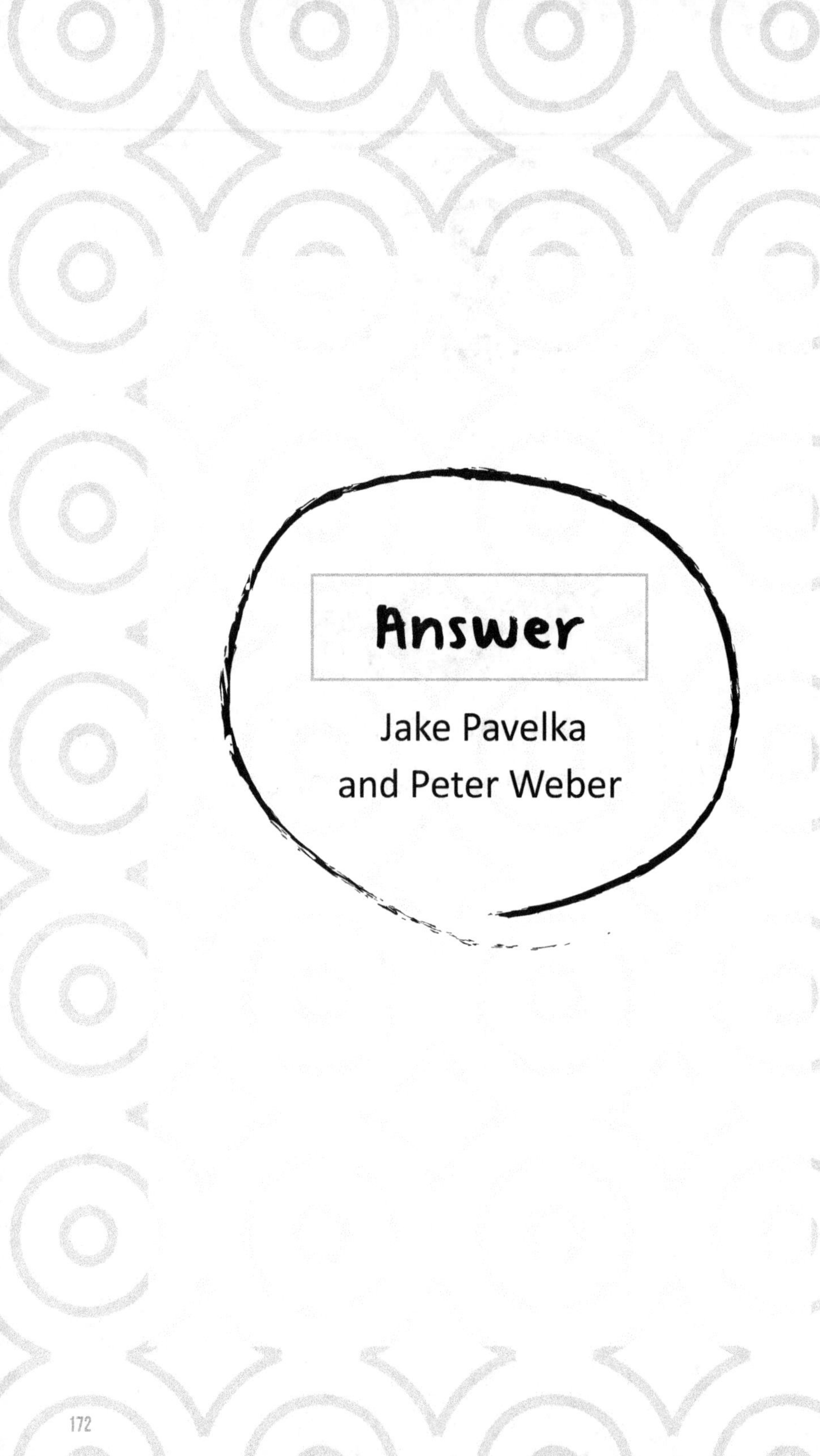
Answer
Jake Pavelka
and Peter Weber

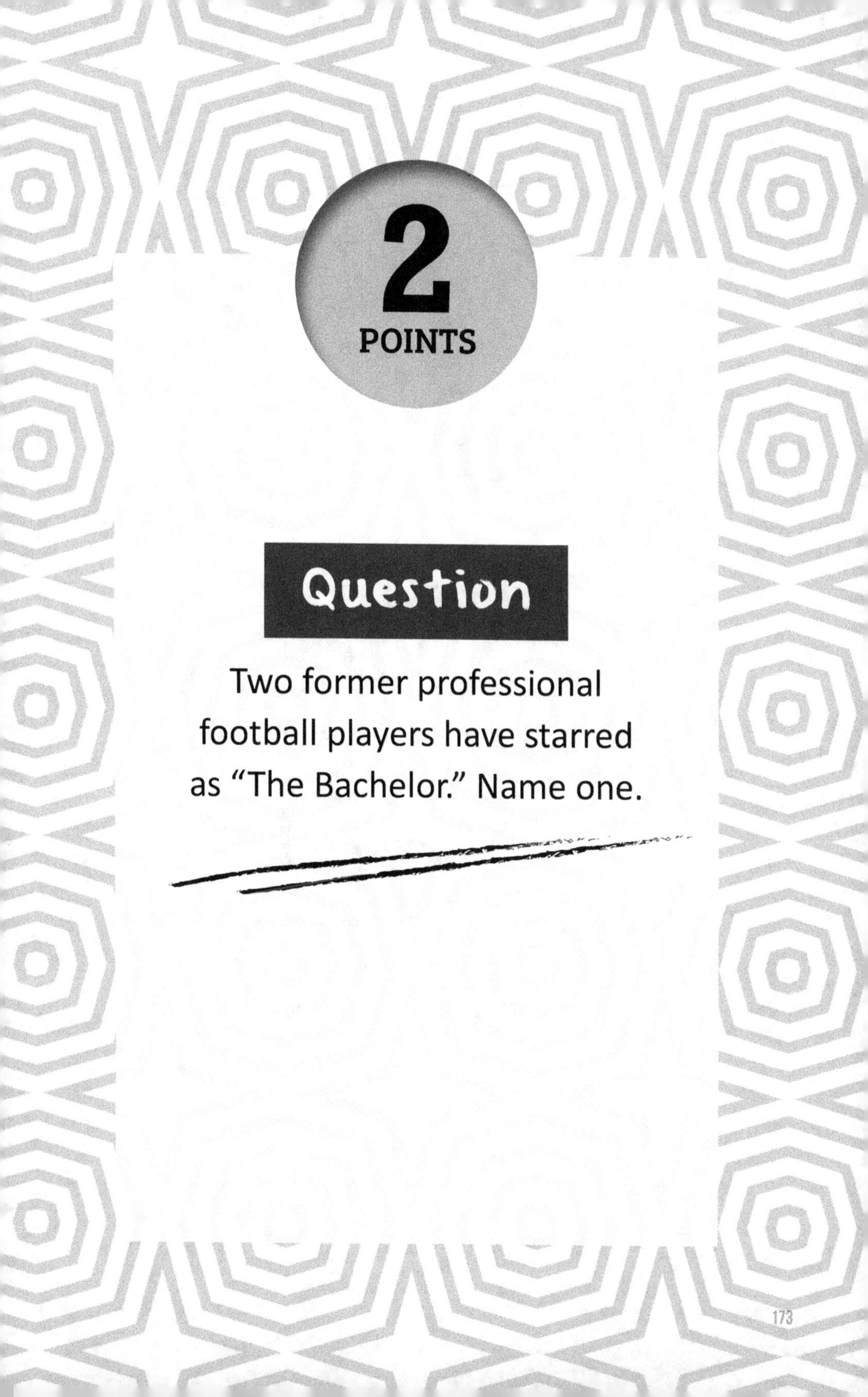

Question

Two former professional
football players have starred
as "The Bachelor." Name one.

Answer

Jesse Palmer and
Colton Underwood

Question

"The Bachelor" star Andy Baldwin worked for what branch of the U.S. military?

Answer

U.S. Navy

Tino Franco was briefly engaged to what Bachelorette after claiming her final rose?

Answer

Rachel Recchia

Question

Susie Evans rejected this Bachelor but later reunited with him.

Answer

Clayton Echard

Question

Who did Hannah Godwin
get engaged to on "Bachelor
in Paradise"?

Answer

Dylan Barbour

Question

Through 2021, which contestant has the greatest number of appearances on different shows within the franchise?

Answer
Chris Bukowski (6)

Question

Before starring as "The Bachelorette," who did Clare Crawley get engaged to after meeting on "Bachelor Winter Games"?

Answer

Benoit Beauséjour-Savard

BONUS
Round!

(Hope you haven't had too much champagne.)

BONUS Round!

You have 30 seconds to act out a contestant from any show in the franchise. You may use words as part of your performance. However, you cannot use the names of **any** specific contestant. If you successfully complete this task, you earn 4 points, and the person who guesses your character correctly earns 1 point.

Question

What couple won the first season of "Bachelor Winter Games"?

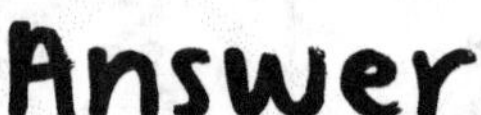

Answer

Ashley Iaconetti
and Kevin Wendt

Question

Two former stars of "The Bachelorette" stepped in to host "The Bachelor" after Chris Harrison left the show. Name one.

Answer

Tayshia Adams and
Kaitlyn Bristowe

2
POINTS

Which contestant did Peter Weber meet before filming began, and eventually date after filming for his season wrapped?

Answer
Kelley Flanagan

Question

Americans Jared Haibon and Grant Kemp appeared on "Bachelor in Paradise" in what country besides the United States?

Answer

Australia

Question

Fill in the blank: "Should you choose to ________ your individual rooms ..."

Forgo

Question

Which former contestant on "The Bachelorette" is best friends with Matt James?

Answer

Tyler Cameron

Question

Which former star of "The Bachelorette" later appeared on "Dancing with the Stars" and "Celebrity Dating Game"?

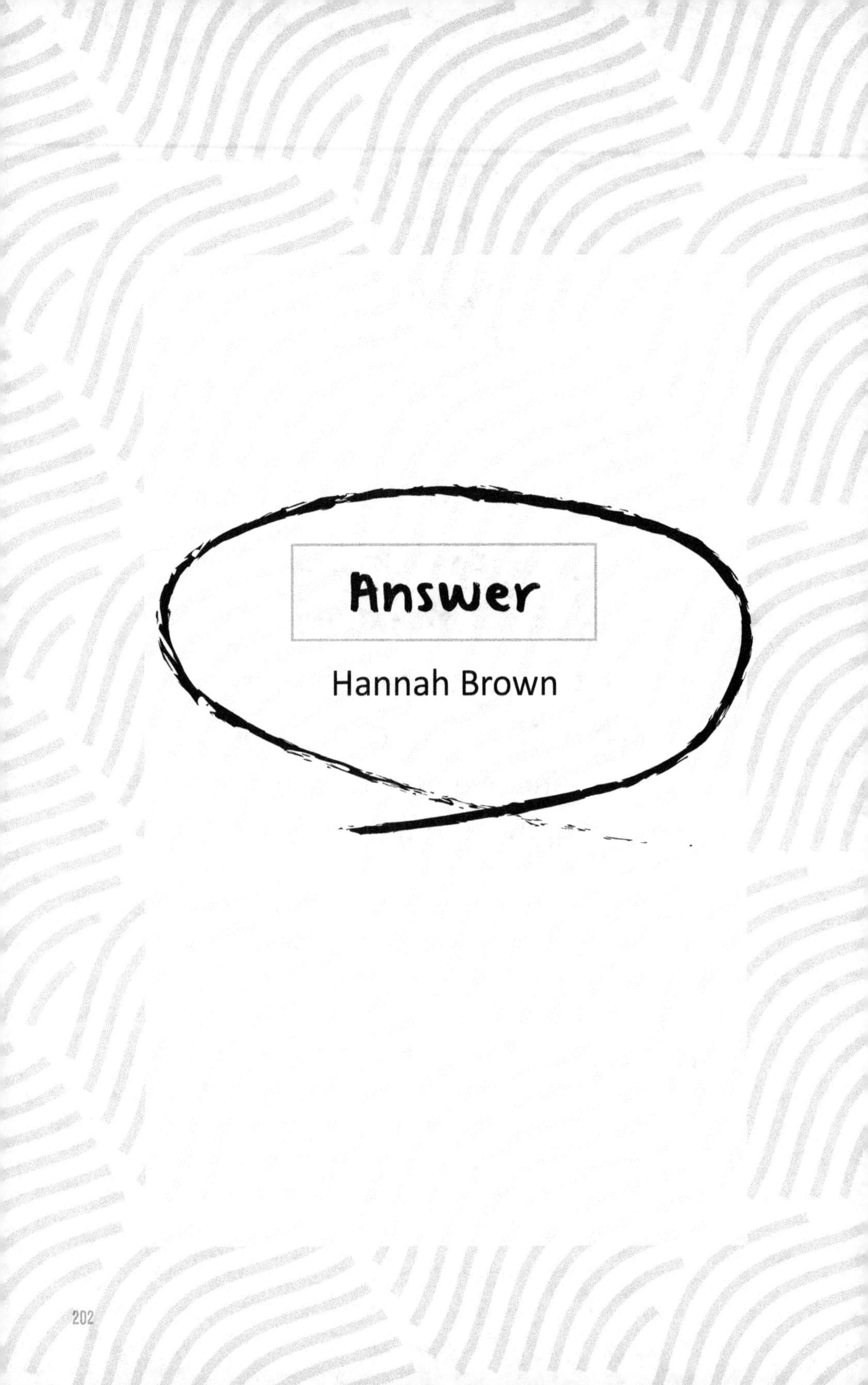

Answer

Hannah Brown

Question

In the first 25 seasons of "The Bachelor," how many stars got married to the woman selected at the Final Rose Ceremony?

Answer

One

(Sean Lowe)

Thank You!

The purchase of this book supported
a small business. We hope you enjoyed it!